C000149279

The Crit

The Crit

An Architecture Student's Handbook

Edited by

Charles Doidge with Rachel Sara and Rosie Parnell

Cartoons by Mark Parsons

AMSTERDAM • BOSTON • HEIDELBERG • LONDON • NEW YORK • OXFORD
PARIS • SAN DIEGO • SAN FRANCISCO • SINGAPORE • SYDNEY • TOKYO

Architectural Press is an imprint of Elsevier

Architectural Press
An imprint of Elsevier
Linacre House, Jordan Hill, Oxford OX2 8DP
200 Wheeler Road, Burlington, MA 01803

First published 2000
Reprinted 2004

Copyright © 2000, Elsevier Ltd. All rights reserved

No part of this publication may be reproduced in any material form (including
photocopying or storing in any medium by electronic means and whether
or not transiently or incidentally to some other use of this publication) without
the written permission of the copyright holder except in accordance with the
provisions of the Copyright, Designs and Patents Act 1988 or under the terms of
a licence issued by the Copyright Licensing Agency Ltd, 90 Tottenham Court Road,
London, England W1T 4LP. Applications for the copyright holder's written
permission to reproduce any part of this publication should be addressed
to the publisher

Permissions may be sought directly from Elsevier's Science & Technology Rights
Department in Oxford, UK: phone: (+44) 1865 843830, fax: (+44) 1865 853333,
e-mail: permissions@elsevier.co.uk. You may also complete your request on-line via
the Elsevier homepage (http://www.elsevier.com), by selecting 'Customer Support'
and then 'Obtaining Permissions'

British Library Cataloguing in Publication Data
Doidge, Charles
    The crit: an architecture student's handbook
    1. Architecture – Study and teaching – Great Britain
    I. Title II. Sara, Rachel III. Parnell, Rosie
    720.7'11'41

Library of Congress Cataloguing in Publication Data
The crit: an architecture student's handbook/edited by Charles Doidge with Rachel
Sara and Rosie Parnell; cartoons by Mark Parsons.
    p. cm.
Includes bibliographical references and index.
ISBN 0 7506 4770 1
    1. Architectural design–Study and teaching–Handbooks, manuals, etc. 2.
Architectural design–Evaluation–Handbooks, manuals, etc. 3. Architectural studios
–Handbooks, manuals, etc. 4. Communication in architectural design–Handbooks,
manuals, etc. I. Doidge, Charles. II. Sara, Rachel. III. Parnell, Rosie.
NA2750.C75
721–dc21   00–038977

ISBN 0 7506 4770 1

For information on all Architectural Press publications
visit our website at www.architecturalpress.com

Composition by Scribe Design, Gillingham, Kent
Printed and bound in Great Britain by Antony Rowe, Chippenham, Wiltshire

Contents

Foreword

The mysteries of the 'jury', 'crit', or 'review' have been enshrined in design education for over a century. Projects and reviews introduced 'learning-by-doing' into design education at the Ecole des Beaux Arts (School of Fine Arts) in Paris in the 1890s and they continue to hold centre stage into the twenty-first century. For hundreds of thousands of students around the world, the design project has been, and remains, the primary method of learning and, in one form or another, culminates in reviews.

Despite its centrality, this 'vital learning vehicle' (if you believe tutors) or 'boring waste of time, ego-trip for staff' (if you believe students) appears to take place without the benefit of a student guide. Students are expected to learn the rules of the game without a rule-book and initiation into this ritual can be a painful rite of passage.

Authors have visited this territory before and, in particular, Kathryn H. Anthony's wide-ranging *Design juries on trial – the renaissance of the design studio* offers an excellent overview. However, this 'seriously useful guide' is believed to be the first aimed primarily at students. It is written and illustrated by recent graduates with their student experiences still vivid in their minds.

Many students think of 'the crit' as an ordeal devised by tutors to leave them feeling as though they have been 'undressed in public'. This need not be the case. This guide shows how to prepare for the rigours of the 'traditional crit' and suggests other less confrontational models including student-led reviews. Instead of thinking of the design review as the 'judgement seat', it can be developed as a celebratory experience.

This guide describes the game, identifies the rules, and advises on tactics. It is a survival guide to help unravel the mysteries and offers practical advice and clarifies objectives. It suggests a more rewarding model appropriate to a 'new professionalism' that is less arrogant and sees clients and users as creative partners in the design process. This was one of the significant outcomes of the recent Clients and Users in Design Education (CUDE) Project in the Sheffield and Leicester Schools of Architecture.

We recommend this book to all design students and particularly to architecture students. It invites and challenges students to be partners, rather than passive recipients, in their educational processes. It can go further and prepare students to be catalysts of the same processes with future clients. It is hoped that design tutors might even take a sneak look at this guide as well and discover with their students that it is never too late to learn.

Professor George Henderson
Head of The Leicester School of Architecture,
De Montfort University
President of the Commonwealth Association of Architects

Professor Jeremy Till
Head of the School of Architecture,
The University of Sheffield

Leicester and Sheffield, January 2000

Acknowledgements

This guide is indebted to numerous tutors, practising architects, fellow students and other writers who have taught, learned, shared experiences and contributed ideas. In thanking them for their inspiration and sometimes provocation, we would like to stress that the views are essentially those of the authors.

The catalyst was a project called 'Clients and Users in Design Education' (CUDE) sponsored by the HEFCE (Higher Education Funding Council for England) fund for the development of teaching and learning. CUDE was initiated in 1996 by John Worthington of the Institute of Advanced Architectural Studies at York, Professor Bryan Lawson at the University of Sheffield School of Architecture, and Professor George Henderson and Judy Ashley at The Leicester School of Architecture, De Montfort University. The project included enhancing student skills of listening, communication and teamwork, through a collaborative rather than confrontational approach to learning.

CUDE was directed in the latter stages by Simon Pilling with support from Angela Fisher, Dr David Nicol, Martin Brookes and Andrew Cooper. To Simon goes the credit for negotiating this guide through its initial stages.

At Sheffield, CUDE was co-ordinated by Angela Fisher, with workshops developed by Simon Pilling, Susan Stern and Martin Brooks. The 'in-school' team was Derek Trowell, Mary Roslin, Helena Webster, Dan Wrightson, Pru Chiles, Russel Light, Eammon Canniffe,

Simon Gedye, Dr Roger Harper, Judy Torrington, and Professor Peter Tregenza.

At Leicester, Judy Ashley died of cancer early in the project and subsequent work was co-ordinated by Jos Boys and Ross Wilmott. The Leicester 'in-school' team included Professor George Henderson, Revd Dr Charles Doidge, Dr Tim Brindley, Mel Richardson, Tony Archibold, Dr Sahap Cakin, Richard Short, Mike Ashley and others, with Dr Margaret Wilkin as external educational consultant.

A special 'thank you' is due to Mark Parsons whose inspiring cartoons and rugged handsomeness have kept the authors going; they have even admitted that they would buy the book for the cartoons alone! It is hoped that the humour and detail will reinforce their poignant messages.

This is an evolving tale and the authors will be pleased to receive comments and anecdotes, via their universities, for possible inclusion in subsequent publications.

This book is dedicated to Theres, Louis, Steve, and Kim.

Introduction

This book should be called 'a study of the blatantly obvious'. It is mostly common sense and, if you stopped to think about it for long enough, I'm sure you could write a very similar guide yourself. The thing is that few of us *ever* stop to think about the point of our crits and we are expected to master them through trial and error. By the time you do master the crit, it is too late!

This book aims to demystify the process, and provide a practical, hands-on guide – how to survive in the current system and then how to begin to change that system.

The crit, or 'review', as we are going to call it throughout this guide, is a feature of studio-based design courses. The design studio is an unusual kind of beast in the university environment and is the part of an architecture course that generally takes up the most time and effort. Typically a design project is set and students are given a limited amount of time to explore it and present their 'ideas' or 'solution' at a review. Other aspects of the course, such as history, technology, design theory, etc. are intended to feed into the studio project. For most of us, the review is unlike any previous experience.

The role of the review has been the focus of recent appraisal (Hall Jones 1996, Anthony 1991, Wilkin 1999). What is the purpose of the review? Should we continue with them at all? Do students learn anything from them? How do they relate to professional practice? This guide does not attempt to extend the theoretical debate but, instead, makes explicit the negative aspects and then the potential value of 'traditional' review and suggests ways to improve performance and learning. We also suggest a range of alternative reviews which you can implement yourself.

It is a 'how to' rather than a theoretical kind of book, but certain changes to the review are implicit – changes which work towards a new professional attitude of inclusiveness, participation and collaboration. We acknowledge the viewpoint that many professionals develop a 'tacit knowing-in-action' (Schön, 1983) and that it is not always possible to articulate this knowledge fully. We do not aim to provide a rule-book, but a framework for thinking about the review within which you can develop your own approach.

Rosie Parnell

My first experience of a review was heart-pumping; it was unlike anything else I had ever had to do but I was expected to just get on with it along with the rest of the year. Okay, so it was interesting to see what other people had produced but why did everyone have to stare at me and my pathetic bits of collapsing cardboard and masking tape and those terrible drawings...ouch! My non-architect friend had inspired me with confidence just before by telling me that my first creation, my pride and joy, looked like a great big toilet roll. So all in all, the whole excruciating experience felt like a perverted form of punishment.

As time went on and I thought I was turning into a bit more of an architect (started wearing more black etc.), the review became an accepted event at the end of each project. My voice still insisted on disappearing into my shoes every time it happened so that I sounded like a Dalek, but with a bit of experience behind me I felt marginally more confident. Unfortunately my marks didn't seem to reflect this, and after each review I would be relieved to be able to begin a new project saying, 'This time, this is the one, this is going to be great!' I still didn't really stop to think, 'What are reviews all about?'

During the Diploma years, Rachel Sara and I worked together, first on short projects with others and then on a year-long project as a pair. It was a great experience. We developed a method of working which seemed to be very efficient, at least judging by the funny looks we got every week from our colleagues when we said that we were going off to London for the weekend, or going to our pottery night class; it seemed that we had a lot more time off than other people. What is more, much to our amazement, our marks started to climb. Neither of us would claim to be natural designers but by the end of the course, our work was being nominated for the RIBA Silver Medal. What was going on here? To this day, all we can think is that our working method must have been effective. Now, I know that on the surface this does not seem to be directly related to the review, but in all of our work we were planning, preparing and looking ahead to that review. Everything that we did was part of our preparation for the review presentation and it helped to define our working method.

Through the Diploma experience and through exposure to a research project called 'Clients and Users in Design Education' (CUDE, which explored things like the review, presentation techniques and group work), both as students and researchers, we learned techniques for review management and preparation. Perhaps most importantly, the CUDE project, combined with recent experience as design tutors, has allowed us to recognize the enormous potential of the review process as a learning experience.

Rachel and I are both involved in tutoring part-time, and as a result, we now experience the review from another point of view. It is *so* nice to have the pressure off! However, there is a different pressure to perform. As a tutor I feel I am expected to have an amazing insight to share with every student. It can be really exhausting and frustrating when I just cannot work out what *is* so fundamentally flawed with student X's piece of work, or what is so brilliant about student Y's. I have begun to understand what makes a good review presentation but I would be the first to admit that someone could come along and break all the rules, talk into their shoes, present their work in the style of Donald Duck and yet be convincing. For the rest of us, however, a bit of pre-planning might be a better approach.

So, these days I've graduated to the trendy glasses brigade – I must be feeling fantastically confident! I'm not sure whether that's true, but it is my sincere hope that this guide can help you to make more of your review process, and in so doing make more of your architectural education.

Rachel Sara

For me, the beginning of the architecture course was a terrifying time. I was suddenly deposited in a city I'd never been to before to share a house with people I'd never met. To make matters worse, I seemed to be on a course that involved more work than anyone else's, in a subject that I didn't have a clue about. At the beginning of each project, I'd read through the brief and wonder what on earth it all meant. I then typically spent the first half of the project doing what all first years on other courses were doing (which was anything but work) and the second half of the project frantically trying to 'pull a white rabbit out of the hat' for the review. By the time it got to the actual event I had had so little sleep that I felt like I was swaying. I would end up spending the following week recovering in bed!

The first review I really remember was one where I had produced a model. I had worked entirely on my own at home which I realize now was a terrible idea. Having done an 'all-nighter' to finish off the cardboard monster that I had begun, I left home feeling weird, but fairly happy with my work (it was, after all, my first ever model). When I got to the studio, my heart sank ... I was so mortified by the shameful quality of my work in comparison with that of other students that I burst into tears. The review did not go well.

I do have memories of reviews that went well, but I have to admit that I don't remember ever learning much from the experience. I certainly never asked myself what reviews were for, or what I wanted to get out of them (other than praise, praise, praise!) When it came to other people's work, I have a recollection of the occasional project which the tutors would unanimously deem brilliant. This would instil in me a feeling of extreme jealousy, soon followed by wonderment and confusion. '*Why* was their scheme so good?' I asked myself, but (mistakenly) never stopped to ask anyone else.

The whole thing was a real shock to the system. I had always done well at school, but this was something else. I would feel full of inspiration and excitement at the beginning of each project, coupled with a 'I'm really going to learn from that last project, and this one's going to be brilliant' feeling. But at the end of each project, I would have to face up to the fact that yet again, my work was not 'brilliant'. My marks were generally reasonable, but I couldn't help thinking that if only I had done a more normal subject (like English or Maths!) I would be doing so much better.

It wasn't until I came back to study for the Diploma that things started to fall into place. I realized that studying architecture was a fantastic opportunity for me to explore issues that really interested me. Architecture suddenly seemed to be relevant to *everything* and I loved it (particularly when I realized that all-nighters weren't compulsory)!

At the end of the Diploma course, I began working in practice part-time. I found myself having to explain work to the client and really having to sell the work that I had done. It took me a while to realize that I could apply my experience with reviews to these situations. I also got involved in participatory design sessions with various groups. I found it really refreshing to 'talk architecture' without the jargon; it was a completely different experience from anything I had done at university. After spending so many years learning to design to my own and my tutors' agendas, it was a totally different thing to incorporate the users' views into my work. Why hadn't I done this in my education? The CUDE project was an excellent opportunity to look at how clients and users might be introduced into future architectural education.

No description of the architecture course can really express what it is like to be an architecture student. But be assured, there are people all over the world who feel as confused, excited, terrified, inspired and challenged as you do. I hope this guide makes you think about reviews – even if it just makes you stop and think about the blatantly obvious for a minute.

Mark Parsons is a recent graduate of the Sheffield University School of Architecture now working in practice.

Charles Doidge was formerly leader of undergraduate architecture at The Leicester School of Architecture, De Montfort University.

Format

The book is formatted to include cartoons, quotations and background information (in grey) alongside the main body of the text. The quotations recall what many remember only too well, and are drawn from interviews carried out by the authors, comments made by Rachel Sara (RS) and two others texts as referenced.

What is a review? 1

1 What is a review?

Synopsis

This guide begins with a look at the what and why of reviews. The review process is introduced and the different types of review held at various stages are described with examples. The potential value of the review and the possible negative aspects are explored. The review at its worst is exposed and contrasted with the best case. Within this framework, the role of the tutor is discussed and the potential role of a participant is explored.

What is a review?

'Excellent fun! I always thought they were a bit like a sport – sparring or jousting. They were usually unnecessarily aggressive affairs, but all done in good humour among a group of friends.' *Practising architect*

'It's a deadline.' *Final year student*

Crit, jury, or review; whichever term you recognize, the quotations show that people have widely differing views of the experience. So what is it exactly?

If you heard the terms 'jury' and 'crit' for the first time you'd probably presume, quite understandably, that they described something negative – maybe even something downright unpleasant. **'Is a jury going to put you on trial?'** (see cartoon 1). Is a crit simply criticizing? These terms don't imply that there is a positive side to the review process. But there is! The review has great potential as a learning experience and this is the reason that it is a firmly established part of most architecture courses. This guide is

Cartoon 1
'Is a jury going to put you on trial?'

'It's an evaluation of the work that's been done.' *Tutor*

'A pointless event, unnecessarily negatively critical.' *Practising architect*

'It's partly an assessment of the project but also controlling a meeting, presentation in public and other useful skills.' *Tutor*

'A chance to get the sleep you didn't get the night before.' *Architecture graduate*

called *'The Crit'* because that term is familiar to most people but we use the term 'review' throughout to promote the more positive aspects of the process.

Your review will vary according to your school, personalities involved and the stage you have reached. When you stop to think about the review and its function, you will realize that it is a surprisingly complex beast. It might be helpful to outline the sort of things you should expect.

Outline of reviews

- Reviews are held both during and at the end of a design project.
- You will present your work and ideas on your own or in a group.
- It could be informal or formal – a chat around a table or **'a presentation to rows of seated individuals'** (see Diagram 1).
- You will usually present a visual and verbal explanation of your work.
- Yours will be one in a series of presentations.
- You will probably have a limited amount of time.
- The audience could be small or large, students in the same year as you, students from other years, tutors involved in teaching the project, other tutors, architects and specialists, or lay-people such as clients and users.
- The audience may give you feedback on your work and discuss ideas with you and each other.
- There is the potential for you to learn from everyone involved.
- You might be marked during the review.

Diagram 1
A presentation to
rows of seated
individuals

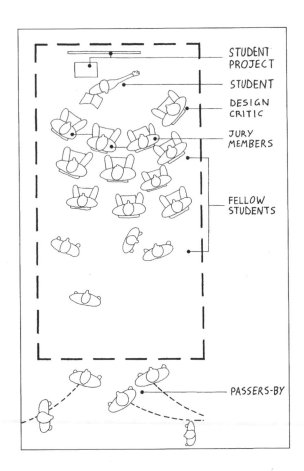

The review stages

Initial stages

You might be expected to discuss the findings of any research you have done with other students and tutors, or even to make a formal presentation. This is the perfect opportunity to learn from others and to bounce around your initial ideas.

Forms of review most likely at this stage:

- Round-table discussion with students and/or tutors.
- Small/medium group tutorial with your tutor(s).

- Meeting with clients or users.
- Question and answer session with an expert, e.g. an engineer.

The review in the Ecole des Beaux Arts

The Ecole des Beaux Arts, founded in 1819, was the leading centre of architectural education in France (Crinson and Lubbock, 1994: 76) and is seen by many architectural educators as an early precursor to the model of architectural education we experience today.

The design problem was developed as the main method of teaching architecture and the review was used as a way of evaluating work. These reviews were carried out behind closed doors by design tutors with no input from students. Since the mid-twentieth century, this process has evolved into an open format. In contrast to the original system, the open, public nature of reviews today is fundamental to the process (see Anthony, 1991: 19).

Intermediate stages

Most design projects involve a presentation of 'work in progress' (an *interim* review). Up to this point you might have discussed your work only in one-to-one tutorials or with friends. An interim review allows you to present your work to a larger audience and get a variety of opinions from your peers and tutors. You could be looking for inspiration or you might want specific advice on how to progress.

Forms of review most likely at this stage:

- Round-table presentation.
- Small/medium group tutorial.
- Formal spoken presentation to a group with work on display.

Final reviews

The *final* stage of the review process is likely to be more formal than earlier stages; this is why it can be the most nerve-wracking stage, particularly if you know that your work is being marked. Like the interim, you can get feedback and learn from the discussion. The principles you learn here can be applied later. In the final review there might also be an emphasis on practising presentation skills for your future life as an architect.

Form of review most likely at this stage:

- Formal spoken presentation to group with reference to work on display.
- Exhibition of work with no verbal presentation.

Review scenarios

'Reviews are there to build a mutual respect – they're a public forum.' *Tutor*

Review: best case

When the review process is working well, it provides many learning opportunities:

- **A chance to evaluate work.** Reviews are never purely a chance to mark work. They provide an opportunity for you to view your own

'It should be a learning process and a common shared airing of the knowledge gained from the project.' *Tutor*

'It should be an appraisal or discussion of your work. You need constructive criticism – this needs to be positive as well as negative. We all need encouragement.' *Practising architect*

'It's an opportunity to get the year's opinions on your work. It gives you a forum for expressing your ideas.' *Student*

work in relation to the work of your peers, consider your rate of progress, and the rate of progress of the class. They enable tutors to evaluate the success of the studio programme, and how well you are working within it.

- **Providing feedback.** Feedback from the review should give you specific instruction on strengths and weaknesses, successes and missed opportunities.
- **Fulfilling project objectives.** It is your chance to show how you have achieved the objectives of the project. It is also an opportunity to explain your *own* objectives in doing the work. If you do not make these clear you can only be judged according to the objectives of your audience.
- **Practise for practice.** The process of presenting to an audience, listening to presentations and forming questions can help you develop skills that are important in architectural practice. The review should help you to build confidence in selling yourself and your ideas.
- **A safe environment.** Despite the link with practice, the school environment gives the advantage of being able to test ideas without the consequences of the real world.
- **Developing critical awareness.** Getting involved in discussion about projects is a good way to develop skills in critical thinking. By trying to understand the different ideas and approaches that you see, you will develop your own thinking about architecture.
- **Learning from *everyone*.** Participating in a review gives you the chance to learn from everyone around you. Students, tutors and other contributors such as specialists, practising architects and lay-people, can provide useful criticism.
- **A focus.** *'At least the crit means we will have finished the project – I'm sick to death of it.'* The review is a deadline which is good practice in time management. Final reviews

provide a ceremonial end to a project, a celebration of your hard work.

Similarities with other fields

Architecture students are not the only ones who have publicly to justify their work. Students in all design fields undergo this process. A similar system is also used in the education of doctors. Medical students are presented with a patient, asked to diagnose their illness and suggest appropriate treatment. Students are then expected to justify their decisions to a reviewing panel. In medicine there is usually only one correct diagnosis and a limited range of treatments and causes, whereas in architecture there are endless solutions to design problems. The review in architecture differs in that its purpose is not to test you in identifying signs; it is an opportunity to develop skills to see possible outcomes.

'I watched a professor pick his nose during a student's entire presentation.' *Student* (Anthony, 1991: 34)

'I've seen jurors fight with one another.' *Student* (Anthony, 1991: 34)

'I was basically, in a very unprofessional way, told that I was stupid and in the wrong field.' *Student* (Anthony, 1991: 34)

'First of all the tutor had the cheek to draw fruit all over someone's elevations, he then proceeded to rip drawings off the wall.' *Student*

'They change according to the time of year, from relatively calm steering groups to abject bollockings later on.' *Practising architect*

Review: worst case

The following list describes a review when it is not working well:

- crowded
- can't see the work presented
- chance to read your magazines
- battering by tutors
- students reduced to tears
- no student debate
- boring, endless...
- tutors only talking about their interests, e.g. public toilets 1876–1877
- so much jargon the presentations might as well be in Martian
- presentations that say the same thing again and again
- aggressive tutors, defensive students

and the list goes on .....

'HEALTH WARNING – REVIEWS CAN SERIOUSLY DAMAGE YOUR HEALTH' (see cartoon 2).

The rest of this guide will provide you with advice on how to either deal with or avoid elements of the worst-case review.

The tutor's role

'I remember one project where a tutor had suggested that I try using a tensile roof structure to cover the shelter I was designing. So, off I went and developed that idea, only for her to tell me in the crit, just how much the roof had spoiled the whole scheme! I learnt that ideas tutors give you are just that – they are ideas to be explored, and not necessarily solutions or answers.' *RS*

'They should be steering you in the right direction rather than telling you what to do.' *Practising architect*

'It's not a demolition job, it's a construction job.' *Tutor*

'A good teacher is an enabler who gives the students a feeling of control of the situation.' *Tutor*

Many students will have come from a school environment where teachers are expected to know all the answers. Coming from this background, it can seem hard to believe that tutors don't have an 'ideal-solution-for-project-4a' hidden up their sleeve. If tutors are not there to provide you with the answers, what exactly should they do?

Tutor's role: best case

In a best-case review, the role of the tutor is as follows.

- **To define the purpose of the review.** If the purpose of the review is clearly defined from the outset, e.g. assessment, learning, presentation practice, or a combination of these, then you know where you stand. Confrontation can be avoided and you are more likely to feel confident (Wilkin, 1999).
- **To provide expert knowledge.** As someone with more experience, a tutor can provide you with insights and valuable knowledge.
- **To enable the learning process.** As an enabler, a tutor can provide situations in which you can learn from your peer group. They can initiate discussion or provide a structure for debate. Tutors should encourage students towards 'self-learning'.
- **To ensure that important issues, relevant to the project, are covered.** The project brief will specify relevant issues and educa-

Cartoon 2
'HEALTH WARNING – REVIEWS CAN SERIOUSLY DAMAGE
YOUR HEALTH'

tional aims. The tutor should make sure that all of these issues are included in the review discussion. If other issues become important due to an individual's approach, the tutor can widen the discussion.

- **To ensure a compromise between equality and flexibility.** It can be very frustrating to see reviews that are twice as long as yours or which focus on completely different issues. It seems unfair. It is up to the tutor to make sure that each student is given similar attention. However, it is often not that simple; if you are going to learn from the review, then it is often most effective to focus on the exceptional and interesting work. This is not very helpful to a tutor who is trying to treat everyone equally and it is confusing to you as student when you have spent two weeks exploring x and y and now the tutor is discussing z! It is up to the tutor to strike a balance.
- **To ensure that the same references are used by all tutors if they are marking work.** With large student numbers in many schools, the reviews may be divided into groups which are run in parallel. To provide a just marking system, the different tutors need to agree on the criteria by which they will judge work.

Tutor's role: worst case

Okay, so tutors are not always as supportive as they could be.

In defence of the tutors, it is important to understand the difficulty of their position. They are expected to concentrate for hours on end, extract the essence of the work presented and come up with profound statements for every piece. It is understandable that tutors sometimes revert to talking about what they know. **'Some tutors feel that they are being judged'** (see cartoon 4) as much as you are.

'Depending on which tutor you had it could be a positive experience with constructive criticism or more confrontational for the sake of it.'
Practising architect

'It could be like sitting in a church, but tutors usually turn it on for the crowds. "They'd drift off into their own experiences"' (see cartoon 3). *Practising architect*

Cartoon 3
'They'd drift off into their own experiences...'

Cartoon 4
'Some tutors feel that they are being judged...'

'Sometimes I feel stupid. You are expected to say something knowledgeable about everyone's work'
Tutor

Most tutors are dedicated educationalists who really want the best for their students, even if you see it differently. Remember that tutors are only human too. Whatever the situation, it is up to you to make the most of the tutor.

Your tutor wants you to do well, not least because they feel that your work is a reflection of their ability.

Your role

The review might sound daunting. You are put on the spot, perhaps alone, and expected to justify your work to a group of people who might not be sympathetic to your ideas. It is unpredictable and you will have to think on your feet. You have to provide the substance for discussion. Nevertheless, this is an opportunity to express your ideas and learn from tutors and fellow students. You can take control, initiate discussion, contribute to the debate and ask for the advice you need.

This is what is expected of you:

- To give people an understanding of your work.
- **'To be clear and interesting'** (see cartoon 5).
- To listen.
- To be open and responsive to learning.
- To contribute to discussion and debate.

The rest of this guide describes your role in the review process in greater depth – in the end **the review is what *you* make it.**

Summary

- The review is a learning experience.
- The review allows you build your presentation skills for later life in practice.
- Participation in review discussion can develop your understanding of architecture.

Cartoon 5
'To be clear and interesting'

Cartoon 6
'... to hear a variety of opinions and ideas about your work'

- The review allows you **'to hear a variety of opinions and ideas about your work'** (see cartoon 6).
- The review allows you to see other people's work and develop critical thinking.
- The review is what you make it.

Before a review: **2**

2 Before a review

Synopsis

This chapter explores the preparation that is needed to do a review and how to go about it. The type of presentation is discussed with reference to the purpose of the review, the target audience, what you want to get out of it, what the audience wants to get out of it and whether you are presenting as an individual or a group. The process of planning and developing the presentation is outlined including time planning, group working and preparing the presentation as a whole through storyboards, words and graphics. The importance of practising a presentation is emphasized. Preparation for the review is introduced as a process that can enable you not only to do better in the review itself, but also to structure the entire project.

Why prepare?

'Even the best ideas need to be sold. And part of selling good products is communicating what's good about them...' *Practising architect (Anthony, 1991: 65)*

'On the couple of times I've had the time to prepare (for a review) I've done a better job and been much calmer.' *Student*

In the run-up to a review, most people spend their time frantically trying to finish all their drawings, **'getting very little sleep in the process'** (see cartoon 7). It is easy to put preparation for the review on hold while you 'just finish this, and start to render that...' As a result, your work can appear to be a complete jumble which is only confused further by your verbal presentation! If you take time out to plan your presentation, the limited time you have can be used far more productively.

Cartoon 7
'... getting very little sleep in the process'

Planning ensures that you spend your time only doing the work that is significant, rather than trying to finish everything you have started.

Working through the night
The 'all-nighter' is a common phenomenon in schools of architecture. If you have the misfortune to find yourself working through the night, remember, you are not alone. The famous Ecole des Beaux Arts had a word for it in the 1890s, 'charrette'. Students worked in attic rooms around Paris and their projects were collected by hand-cart, a charrette. As it clattered down the cobbled street, even if you had been at it all night, there was always something last-minute that still had to be done.

How to prepare

What to think about

Preparing for a presentation involves making conscious decisions. Write down your responses to these questions:

- Who is presenting?
- Who are you presenting to?
- How long have you got?
- Where are you presenting?
- How much space have you got?
- What is the purpose of the review?
- What are the main ideas/concepts that you want to get across?
- How does your work connect with existing knowledge?
- How have you addressed the aims and objectives of the project?
- What do *you* want to get out of it?

Who is presenting?

If you are presenting alone, consider your own strengths and weaknesses, both in terms of visual

'One of the projects I did was in the middle of a beautiful summer. The weather was fantastic, and I couldn't bear to be inside. So I vowed to do all of the work in the garden and to really enjoy myself. I spent the time painting and, of course, the fact that I'd really enjoyed myself came across in the work. The review went brilliantly.' *RS*

and verbal presentation. There is no point in planning a presentation in delicate water-colour when you are a marker pens and crayons person.

For a group presentation, you need to spend plenty of time planning who is going to do what. Again, this needs to be tailored to the strengths and weaknesses of each individual. Who are the confident speakers? Who would be most suited to presenting a prepared text? Both visually and verbally, each individual's work needs to be made part of a cohesive whole through careful planning.

A successful presentation ties together the visual and the verbal presentations of the project in one cohesive whole.

Who are you presenting to?

'Who is the target audience' (see cartoon 8) and what will they want to get out of the session? When presenting, it is easy to get so self-absorbed that you forget about the people in front of you. It is reasonable to expect a degree of architectural knowledge from tutors and fellow students, but presenting to a community group or school group is totally different. Should you use architectural conventions such as plan, section and elevation or more accessible models and sketches? At what level should the verbal presentation be pitched?

Whatever the audience, you have failed if, at the end of your presentation, the audience does not have a clear understanding of your work.

How long have you got?

If you have five minutes, you will have to concentrate on a couple of key ideas. This is excellent practice in self-discipline. You should be able to describe even the most complex of

Cartoon 8
'Who is the target audience ...'

ideas in five minutes. If you have more time, you can go into more detail but **'don't talk about issues that aren't important to the work'** (see cartoon 9). Will anybody really be interested that you spent all of last night trying to fit the toilets into that space? You are bound to have accumulated more information than you have time to present, so be ruthless.

Abraham Lincoln could speak for an hour on any topic but, if you wanted him to speak for three minutes, he needed a day to prepare.

It is up to you to keep your presentation within the agreed time.

Where are you presenting?

If you feel that the atmosphere of the space is essential to the presentation or you need different facilities, then you might be able to organize another venue; most tutors will be impressed that you have shown the initiative.

How much space have you got?

Plan the arrangement of work (drawings, models etc.) so that people can read the story in a logical way. Stand at the distance of the furthest observer and think about what they have to see.

What is the purpose of the review?

If you are not sure, you should ask your tutor to clarify this, e.g. is the main purpose of this review to practise presentation skills, to evaluate/mark the project (and is the verbal defence of your work a component in the mark) or to get feedback from peers?

Cartoon 9
'... don't talk about issues that are not important to the work'

Cartoon 10
'Be aware of your own objectives ...'

What are the main ideas/concepts that you want to get across?

Once you have identified the ideas that generated the work, you can use these to tie together the presentation as a whole, visually and verbally. For example, if one of the key ideas that you incorporated into your design for a nursery was the blurring of the boundaries between inside and outside, then make sure your work shows this. You might focus the verbal presentation on the way in which your work has developed from concept to design solution.

How does your work connect with existing knowledge?

Refer your work to something the audience will have experienced – somewhere you've all visited, childhood memories, common experience, etc.

How have you addressed the aims and objectives of the project?

Refer back to any aims and objectives stated in the brief. How have you approached these? Become aware of how the aims and objectives are developing over the course to gain a sense of progress in your learning.

What do you want to get out of it?

'Be aware of your own objectives' (see cartoon 10) when planning the presentation. If it is an interim presentation, feedback is vital. If it is a final presentation, are you only trying to sell your work or do you also want advice on improving it?

How to plan and develop the presentation

So now you have asked yourself the key questions about your review, how do you go about preparing for it? Here are some helpful stages:

- Decide on the format/method/media you will use.
- Design a 'storyboard' for the presentation.
- If you are in a group, decide who will do what, and in what order.
- Make a time-plan working back from your deadline.
- Practise.

Cartoon 11
'Performance art'

Decide on the format/method/media you will use

Options available

Appropriate situations

2D visuals displayed on a wall facing the audience, e.g. drawings, paintings, collage

This sort of presentation should speak for itself, even if you are going to do a verbal presentation as well.

Overhead projector with prepared overheads

Good for a well-structured formal presentation. Can imply a passive audience.

Slide projector

As above but needs careful pre-planning.

Overhead projector where drawing on the overheads is part of the presentation

As above, but drawing on transparencies can help the presentation seem less final and invite more participation. More appropriate if you are good at drawing.

Small-scale models/reports/ drawings to be presented around a table

Suitable for a small group presentation. Particularly good for developing discussion around the work.

3D visuals that need the audience to walk around the presentation

Good if you want to stand out from the crowd. The need to move around the presentation keeps people interested.

Powerpoint or other computer presentation

Most appropriate for formal presentations. Check on equipment.

Computer model displayed on screen

This can allow interactive walk-throughs which are particularly suitable for an audience which doesn't read architectural drawings. However, do not confuse flashy graphics with good design.

Interactive presentation where the audience is expected to participate in the generation of ideas

Particularly appropriate for the involvement of community or school groups but needs to be extremely well planned. Consider using rough models, paint and play-dough etc. Can be an alternative way of approaching university reviews as well.

Film or video played to the audience

Ideal if you are shy. It is an easy way to make sure the presentation is fully pre-prepared but it prevents interaction.

'Performance art' (see cartoon 11), music, dance, poetry, mime, etc.

Ideal if you are still drunk from the night before! This approach can be really unusual and interesting, but if not done well, there is nothing worse than embarrassing yourself and the audience.

Other ideas

Endless possibilities.

Be aware that the more hi-tech the equipment you use, the longer you will need to spend preparing.

Design a storyboard for the presentation

'Good drafting in your speech and good drafting on a piece of paper is the same state of mind.' *Practising architect (Anthony, 1991: 65)*

A storyboard is used in planning a film or advertisement. It consists of **'a "board" which tells a "story" in words and sketches'** (see cartoon 12) and which is the plan for the film or advert. Design your presentation as a combination of key text and sketches. It can be helpful to do this in pairs:

- Write down your 'must-says' (individually).
- Present them to your colleague.
- Get your colleague to tell you what they thought you said.
- Check that the key ideas have been communicated effectively.

Sketch out your storyboard to indicate both the visual and the verbal presentation. Bear in mind all the questions you need to answer. Arrange your 'must-says' in a logical order. Look at the work you have already done, and choose the pieces which best represent each of your key ideas. What else needs to be done to reinforce these points? For example, does the landscape needs to be painted on all the drawings to emphasize its importance? Plan the work in a logical sequence so that viewers are not required to jump around in order to follow your presentation. All your work should be clear and easy to read, even from the back of the audience. Bear in mind the importance of your visual presentation. Whether you like it or not, a study carried out by Lowe (1969) showed that presentation strongly affected the judgements (and hence, marking) of tutors.

It can help to follow a few rules when structuring the presentation. Bear in mind **'the listening curve'** (see Diagram 2), which shows attention over time.

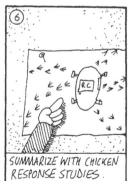

Cartoon 12

'... a "board" which tells a "story" in words and sketches ...'

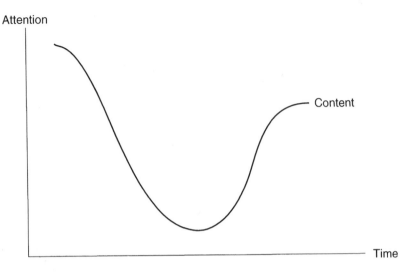

Diagram 2
The listening curve

The classic rule is: 'tell 'em what you're gonna tell 'em, tell 'em, and tell 'em what you told 'em.'

- **The beginning of the talk.** The audience's attention is greatest at this point so, once you have introduced yourself, state your key ideas immediately.
- **The middle section.** Expand on each key idea.
- **The end of the presentation.** The final section of the presentation should restate your key ideas. You may also wish to ask questions. People remember more of the start and finish of a talk than the middle. Be careful to conclude only once and go out with a bang, not a whimper.

If you are in a group, decide who will do what, and in what order

The storyboard will need to include all the members of the group. Make sure you are all clear about who is going to cover what and how each will hand over to the next speaker.

Make a time-plan, working back from your deadline

'If I have a deadline to meet I'm old enough and wise enough now to know how much time it's going to take if everything went well. But I also know that more often than not, everything does not go well. So I try to allow even more time....' *Michael Graves (Anthony, 1991: 46)*

Good time management means that you will get plenty of sleep the night before (if possible!), and as a result will be more confident and able to participate in the review. You might suggest to tutors that everybody submits their work the evening before.

Time management is particularly difficult in design work. A vital leap of creativity might happen at any point – in bed, on your bike, or in the pub. But last-minute changes to the design can have a domino effect on all of the work.

Try using the following tools to help you manage your time:

Plan at the beginning of each week

Make a rough plan of what you want to achieve, including time for socializing.

Use a diary

Write down what tasks you want to accomplish each day.

Prioritize

Do the essential work first.

Plan the next day at the end of the last

At the end of the working day, take five minutes to plan what you are going to do the next day so that when you start work, you will be able to get straight on with it.

Be flexible

Don't worry if you need to re-schedule tasks for another day.

'I had 8 hours left before the review began and all I had to do was finish my drawings. I began on the ground floor plan, and there seemed to be lots of decisions still left to make, so I began drawing the floor tiles in (supposedly while I thought about the other decisions). Of course, once I'd started, I felt I had to finish, which meant that by the time I got to the review, I had nothing to show except some beautifully drawn squares.' *RS*

Don't get side-tracked

Once you have prioritized, don't get side-tracked into doing a low priority task, like drawing all the bathroom tiling before designing the rest of the house.

Divide the work into small manageable tasks

It is much easier to start if you do not feel you are facing a single insurmountable task. A Chinese proverb states, 'The longest journey begins with a single step'.

Work back from your deadline

Don't forget that every task takes three times longer than you estimate.

Give yourself over-run time

Set yourself a deadline a day or so before the real one. That way, you will have some extra time if you are ill, or if the clock runs faster!

Find a workmate

Have regular meetings with a colleague to discuss each other's progress and what you should be doing next. It is useful to have a 'think point', be accountable, and have an outside opinion.

Plan chunks of undisturbed time

'Write a sign saying, "Do not disturb" ...' (see cartoon 13). If anyone tries to disturb you, pass them the appointments book!

Check on yourself

Regularly ask yourself, 'What should I be doing now to make the most of my time?'

Cartoon 13
'Write a sign saying "Do not disturb" ...'

Put aside time for the unexpected

You never know when a friend might be in need, or you might get an unexpected visit or opportunity.

Deal with stress

Make time to exercise and eat properly (when you are stressed you need more nutrients) and keep up non-architectural activities.

Just start!

Starting work is the most difficult part. Give yourself a really easy task to begin with or say to yourself that you are just going to do the work in rough first. Don't be afraid of making mistakes, even huge ones! They are often the best way to learn. **Remember – it doesn't have to be perfect, it just has to be done.**

Practise

Practising the presentation beforehand will make you more confident on the day. Have a run-through with others. Practise on your friends and family or with a video camera or tape recorder, or even a mirror. Focus on the good aspects and be prepared to answer questions on more doubtful aspects of your design.

Take into account the following when practising:

- **Plan your opening sentence.** Start with confidence and direction (perhaps by breaking the ice with a joke).
- **Check the audience understands the key points.** Ask your audience to repeat back to you the essence of what they thought you said. If they get it wrong, then it's back to the verbal drawing board.

- **Imagine questions.** Think up the most diffi-cult questions you could be asked and prepare answers for these.
- **Timing.** Make sure that the planned presen-tation is shorter than the time available.
- **Avoid jargon.** Good communication is about getting across complex ideas in an under-standable way.
- **Experiment with the delivery.** Reading a prepared presentation word-for-word can seem artificial and even boring. Instead, write yourself an outline of the key points. However, if you are extremely shy, or your English is not good, then reading a script may be the best option.
- **Study successful speakers.** What did they do to attract your attention? Was it something funny, very unusual, or did they just have an air of confidence? Even watch-ing TV can count as research! Study TV cooks, weather presenters and so on. Think about the way in which you can apply these ideas to your own presentations.

Speaking 'off-the-cuff' is an expression derived from an actor's practice of having key lines written on the cuff of his shirt. The equiv-alent is to have a series of keywords written on cards or to have a series of diagrams and keywords along the top as part of the display.

You should aim to spend seven times the length of the presentation preparing and practising, i.e. if you are presenting for 10 minutes, you should spend 1 hour and 10 minutes preparing and practising the presen-tation.

Don't be afraid to break all the rules if you believe something strongly enough. You could end up producing something excep-tional.

Professional parallels

'[Every week] I have to present my projects to my clients and to many different groups – boards, advisors, trustees.' *Cesar Pelli (Anthony, 1991: 67)*

Presentation skills are essential for all sorts of professional practice. The formal review has parallels with the high-pressure presentation, which an architect might deliver to a client board deciding who should be commissioned to take on the job. The workplace is competitive and those who pull the purse strings also judge your performance as an architect.

The less formal review might be paralleled by the architect's meeting with the client or user group to develop the brief or design. In this situation, the hard sell is rarely appropriate. Here the client/user-architect relationship is very different and potentially, much more creative. If the architect has an inclusive attitude and has good listening skills, the client can play a key role in the design process.

Even a meeting with the bank manager or a consultant can benefit from skills in presentation. Practising and developing these skills in architecture school will provide you with a good grounding for practice of any sort, and it could certainly come in useful in job interviews.

So now you have prepared and managed your time successfully you can get an early night and feel ready for the day of the review itself. (Yeah, right!)

Summary

- Planning ensures that you spend your time doing work that is appropriate, rather than trying to finish everything.
- Tie together the visual and verbal presentations in a cohesive and logical whole.
- Whatever the audience, you have failed if, at the end of your presentation, the audience does not have a clear understanding and picture of the key ideas of the work.
- Structure the talk with a beginning, middle, and end.
- Consciously manage your time.
- Approximately seven times the length of the presentation should be spent practising.

During a review: **3**

3 During a review

Synopsis

This chapter concentrates on the day of the review. Maximizing the hard work you have put into the presentation period is a key theme. The importance of managing yourself is highlighted and tips are offered on how to prepare yourself psychologically and physically for the presentation. Consideration is given to the props you will require, including setting up equipment, making sure it is working, exhibiting your drawings and models, etc. Various communication skills required for a range of review scenarios are discussed with reference to parallels in practice. Practical guidance is offered in order to build skills in managing the review and in dealing with unexpected situations.

Performing on the day

'The first solo crit was very nerve-wracking and it was difficult to remember what it was you had to say.' *Second year student*

'I would rather go to the dentist's than have a review.' *Third year student (Wilkin, 1999)*

What would you guess was the number-one fear in life of the US population ... death perhaps? Wrong, it's public speaking! So, if reviews are a form of public speaking, as they often are, it is no wonder that most of us find them a little nerve-wracking. In fact, according to one architect, public speaking is the best laxative!

After all that preparation and practice, you want to be sure that you are going to make the most

'I fail to produce stuff in a coherent order because I'm nervous and rarely prepare.'
Second year student

of it on the day itself. Unfortunately most people assume public speaking is about instant humiliation; with all eyes on you, surely things can only go wrong. **'Nerves can be a particular problem'** (see cartoon 14) in formal reviews.

Few people are born presenters and, after years spent in the education system exercising your brain rather than your body and voice, it is unlikely that you will have had much practice. If you have the right approach to the review from the outset, you will be able to develop skills as a convincing performer and as an architect who responds to the client in a creative way that includes the client's views.

Managing yourself

'Your project's only as good as how well you can sell it.' *Final year student*

'Impending doom. I'm very bad at speaking in public and I found crits absolutely terrible.' *Recent graduate*

Your ability to convey your ideas to the audience is vital to the success of your work. When it comes to the effect you have on your audience, it has been suggested that 60 per cent is created by your physicality, 30 per cent by the tone of your voice and the remaining 10 per cent by what you actually say. (But that doesn't mean you can forget about the work itself!) Managing yourself psychologically and physically is vital to a successful performance.

Think about the following:

- **'Body language'** (see cartoon 15). Avoid folded arms (looks defensive), head dropped down (the voice goes with it), slouched shoulders (lack of confidence), fiddling with your hands (distracting), covering your mouth (not telling the truth).
- **Use your body**. The best performers are relaxed and open and are not afraid to use space. Emphasize important points in a flamboyant gesture! Do not feel constrained; the more animated your presentation, the clearer the message.
- **Use your face**. Smile! The more animated your face, the more easily you will hold the

Cartoon 14
'Nerves can be a particular problem'

Cartoon 15
'Body language'

'For the first few crits I was scared to death because I thought that my work was crap.'
Recent graduate

'There's always a danger that crits become a performance ... Performance is like acting, moving outside oneself. A proper presentation is a genuine expression of oneself and one's work.'
Michael Wilford, Architect.

One review degenerated into a full-scale argument. I was so fired up and upset that I felt my heart pounding; I was sure I was going to die. I just about survived, but straight afterwards developed a terrible migraine and was confined to my room for a day or so.'
RS

attention of your audience. Warm it up, slap your cheeks, blow through your lips; just get your face, lips and tongue going so that they are warmed-up ready for performance.

- **Breath control**. Breathing is essential! Breathe steady breaths and your brain will receive more oxygen, you'll have more energy and will feel calmer. Try a breathing exercise just before your presentation.

- **Tone of voice**. Your audience will not find your work interesting if you sound bored by the whole thing. If your voice has some musicality, **'try varying pitch and rhythm'** (see cartoon 16) to convey enthusiasm. Warm your vocal chords before your presentation and have a glass of water to hand in case your voice starts to go.

- **Attitude.** Your attitude to the review can greatly affect your confidence and ability to perform. Focus on the positive before you begin. Don't walk in thinking, **'They're going to hate it'** and set yourself up for failure. Instead think, 'I'm going to share my project with you and I'm going to enjoy it!' Think of the review as an opportunity to share your ideas, gain valuable feedback and engage in interesting discussion, rather than as a time when everyone judges you. Developing this attitude should prepare you for working with clients in a creative and inclusive way.

- **Be yourself.** If you try to perform out of character, you will not feel comfortable and relaxed and your work will lack integrity. Your best hope is to be yourself.

Beat nerves, be yourself
Adrenalin is useful for getting you fired up and focused on the task in hand. If, however, you are going to survive to see the end of your review, you need to be reasonably relaxed. Here are a few suggestions:
- Adopt a relaxed and confident posture and convince yourself that you are calm.

Cartoon 16
'Try varying pitch and rhythm...'

- Focus on what you are doing instead of worrying about what others think.
- Remember that your tutors and other reviewers are only human like you.
- Do not drink caffeine before your presentation.
- Pick a face, make contact and smile!
- Focus on the positive before you present.
- Think, 'I'm going to enjoy sharing my project with you.'
- Do not think of the review as a time to be judged, but a time to engage in interesting discussion.

Checklist

- Focus on the positive.
- **'Have a facial'** (see cartoon 17) and vocal warm-up before you begin.
- Animate your presentation using your face, voice and body.
- Be enthusiastic, smile, be yourself.

Perceptions of the same review

Student	Tutor
I have been up the last three nights slaving away on this project. This jury had better appreciate what I've been through!	Pooh, what's that smell? This person looks as though his hair could be used as a chip pan and his clothes look like he's been living in them for days.
I'm so nervous I don't know if I can even go through with this.	She's had three entire months to work on this crazy project, but she looks scared stiff. What can she possibly be so nervous about?
These ten minutes in the review are the most important minutes of the entire academic term.	Can I possibly last through another ten minutes? I'm getting so uncomfortable in this dreadful chair, plus I'm dying for a wee. I hope this guy talks fast.

(adapted from Anthony, 1991: 76)

Cartoon 17
'Have a facial...'

Managing your talk

'It annoys me when people repeat themselves or talk bollocks.' *Diploma student*

Here are some tips for the day itself:

- **Be prepared to adjust your talk if need be.** **'If your audience is losing interest'** (see cartoon 18), move on to another point or explain in a more interesting way. Do not stick rigidly to your script if you are sending people to sleep.

- **Dealing with interruptions.** Audience interaction often produces a richer presentation, but the discussion can expand into areas that you didn't want to talk about. You can make it clear to the audience at the beginning that you would like to make your presentation without interruption and take questions and comments at the end. Alternatively, be firm and guide the conversation back on track if necessary.

- **Don't begin by apologizing.** How many times have you heard presenters begin by saying 'I am sorry I haven't quite finished but...' or 'You probably can't see on these scrappy drawings.' Start with an aura of confidence, with all that preparation, you should have nothing to apologize for.

- **Don't speak too casually.** Countless 'y'know', 'sort of', 'kind of', 'stuff' comments can make you seem very unprofessional.

- **Avoid pet phrases.** People will focus on these instead of the substance of what you have to say.

- **Avoid sexist/racist stereotypes.** For example, assuming every client is a white male.

- **Don't ramble just to fill up time.** By talking less, your audience may take more in.

- **Speak slowly.** The more slowly you speak, the more information people absorb and the clearer the message.

Cartoon 18
'If your audience is losing interest...'

- **Don't be afraid to say 'I don't know'.** It's better than inventing an answer.
- **Don't finish on a weak point.** Don't peter out saying 'Well, I think that's about it.' Prepare a confident ending and then pause and say 'Thank you'.
- **Face your audience.** It's easy to slip into the habit of talking to your drawings.
- **Make eye contact with the audience.**

Jargon

'The latest word in our studio is 'polemic'. There's a new one every week!' *Diploma student*

'Some people can talk absolute rubbish in a very complicated way. It might sound impressive to start with, but if you listen, it doesn't make any sense.' *Second year student*

Architecture, like any other culture, has developed **'its own vocabulary and jargon'** (see cartoon 19). The parts of a building whose names were once familiar develop a whole host of new terms. Lewis (1998) in his book, *'Architect?'* gives an entertaining account of the lingo you might hear. The following is adapted from his book:

When describing the visual characteristics of a building, architects like to talk about the scale, image, appropriateness and texture. Metaphor is often used to describe an idea or a concept. One can talk about the "typology" of the building, the "circulation", "coherence" and the "layered" elements. A building can be interesting, competent, convincing, ugly or beautiful – and so it goes on.

Space can refer to just about anything from an outside toilet cubicle to New York's Central Park. Space in action can "flow", "penetrate", "articulate", "modulate", "expand" or "contract". It can be amorphous and open, without clear boundaries, or it can be crisply defined, figural and contained, with discernible shape and boundaries. (see Lewis, 1998: 59–81)

Cartoon 19
'... its own vocabulary and jargon'

People	Architect
Buildings	constructs
	habitable artifacts
	environments
	built form
	structures
	edifices
Windows	fenestration
	voids in walls
	oculi
	penetrations
	punched openings
	apertures
	cutouts
Walls	vertical planes
	membranes
	surfaces
	space definers
	enclosing envelopes
	partitions
	separators
Corridors	galleries
	circulation conduits
	pedestrian streets
	passages
	channels
	ambulatories
Courtyard	atrium
	peristyle
	interior open space
Porch	transitional space
	loggia
	portico

(adapted from Lewis, 1998)

Some of these terms and phrases might help you to communicate your ideas more succinctly but others could complicate a point that is really quite simple. Sometimes, an audience will be seduced by complex explanation and long words but overuse of jargon can be a bad habit – **'your future clients are unlikely to have a clue what you are talking about!'** (see cartoon 20).

Presentation bingo!

First person with a full line or column wins:

catch a glimpse of	juxtaposed	and that's about it	kind of
polemic	sort of	narrative	axis
transitional space	a journey	draws you	punctures
pedestrian street	impromptu performance space	floating roof	ran out of time

Managing your audience

Including the audience

The level of interaction with the audience will depend on the type of review, personalities involved, the work itself and the time of day. Don't be afraid to change the set-up of your review if appropriate. If you have some work that requires close inspection, ask people to move their chairs to create a semi-circle around the work, or stand up and come and look.

Encouraging discussion

The discussion that takes place after you speak is usually richer and more useful to you if more people take part. Be proactive and invite people to contribute, particularly other students who usually keep their mouths shut! Sometimes the discussion goes off in an unanticipated direction. This can be a good thing, providing you with a new perspective, or you may find your audience

Cartoon 20
'... your future clients are unlikely to have a clue about what you are talking about!'

talking about something you have chosen not to concern yourself with; in this case, explain your priorities and guide the discussion back to the issues that you feel are most relevant. If you can get used to encouraging discussion and interacting with your audience in reviews, you will be able to encourage clients to discuss ideas with you in the future.

Dealing with confrontation

Not every review will be confrontational, but you need to be prepared to meet this situation. Some personalities react very well and even enjoy responding to confrontation. The rest of us find it intimidating. If you dislike the tone of a comment, or simply disagree with it, try to listen and let the person finish. Take a deep breath and **'try not to react negatively or defensively'** (see cartoon 21) and then check your understanding. If you still disagree with the comment, calmly say so and explain why. This is good practice for possible future encounters with difficult clients; you can't afford to fall out over a misunderstanding or personality clash, and resolving differences can be constructive.

Missiles
Some comments are **'so destructive that they are best ignored'** (see cartoon 22). The following comments and actions are from actual experiences:
- 'My four-year-old son could do better.'
- 'You would be better off selling dresses' (to a female student).
- 'Learn how to speak' (to someone with a strong Essex accent).
- 'Don't you own any pencil crayons?' (when you have used paints for a change).
- 'Your house looks like it's from Noddyland'.
- 'It looks better now!' (as a tutor turned the model upside-down and stood on it).

Cartoon 21
'... try not to act negatively or defensively'

Cartoon 22
'... so destructive that they are best ignored'

Managing your props

Each presentation method will involve a different medium, piece of equipment or 'prop'. It is important that on the day you check any props required. Make sure that all equipment is available and working. Check how to turn on things like computers or projectors, how to adjust volume, etc. Be sure that you are familiar with any equipment that you need and have a quick run through your slides or overheads etc. Make sure that they are in the correct order and not upside-down or back-to-front. If things do go wrong on the day, don't panic – **'audiences are very understanding of technical hitches'** (see cartoon 23) and will be surprisingly patient if need be.

When you are displaying drawings and models etc. make sure that they are positioned carefully for visibility and clarity. If one piece of work contains a lot of information be sure that it is has a prominent position.

Summary

- Managing yourself physically and psychologically allows you to maximize the effort that has gone into your work.
- Your whole body is an instrument for communication.
- You will be more relaxed if you can just be yourself.
- You can guide your review along the path that you would like it to take.
- The review is an opportunity for you to share and discuss your work and ideas, not just a time to be judged!
- Check your work and any equipment etc. on the day.

Cartoon 23
'... audiences are very understanding of technical hitches...'

Learning from a review: 4

4   Learning from a review

Synopsis

This guide seeks to promote the review as a place of learning, emphasizing the rewards to be gained by putting more effort into the experience. This chapter outlines the various ways in which you can learn from the review, highlighting skills you can practise and offering practical tips. The learning opportunities fall into two categories: learning from your own review and learning from the reviews of your peers. Areas covered include learning about your own design from feedback and discussion, learning to think critically about architecture by observing the work of others, participating in discussion, and learning about presentation skills through feedback and observation.

Introduction

'The problem is that there's hardly any discussion among students. It's usually because the work is being marked at the same time, so you don't want to say anything too critical or put their work down.' *Final year student*

'You learn as much or more from everybody else as you do from your tutor.' *Practising architect*

Hopefully you're now convinced that the review can be something other than a terrifying ordeal to be endured, but what about the impact of the review on your work? Potentially, the review plays an important part in your learning, although there is disagreement about whether the review is principally for marking or for learning. It is taken for granted that the *interim* review is for learning – a chance to get feedback on your ideas, which should help you to develop your design further. The status of the *final* review, however, is less clear.

'Interim crits have more value, allowing you to get a variety of feedback – you can stagnate if it's just you and your tutor discussing ideas.' *Final year student*

'Project reviews are for better creative understanding.' *Second year student (Wilkin, 1999)*

Some tutors view the review as an occasion to discuss students' work 'in order to find out how well they've done and that discussion is an assessment process'. Other tutors say adamantly, 'Crits are not assessment' (Wilkin, 1999). This belief is usually associated with concern that marking can diminish the learning potential of a review. Whether or not the review includes marking, you should treat it as an opportunity to learn.

To mark or not to mark?

Some schools mark work after each review whereas others wait until the end of the year to mark everything. In both cases the tutors at reviews are often those who mark the work, so initial evaluation of the work will have inevitably taken place.

The case for marking

A recognized function of the review is to provide you with practice in presenting and selling ideas to a panel such as you might encounter in practice. It can be argued that if work is assessed by a panel of tutors on the basis of what they have seen and heard in the review, then the experience is brought closer to the real world scenario. Another function of the review is to provide you with a deadline and focus for the work – also good practice for the real world. Although there could be a deadline without assessment, the knowledge that your work is going to be marked tends to help you to focus! The attention required for marking also allows many students to feel that their efforts are valued. In our experience this perceived attention to individuals' work by tutors has been sorely missed when assessment has been removed.

The case for removing marking

If marking is one of the functions of the review, learning potential is decreased in a number of ways (Hall Jones 1996, Wilkin 1999). First, students are likely to be more anxious. Mild anxiety might improve performance but too much will reduce the students' ability to retain information. Second, the review as assessment encourages the presentation of work as a final product and avoids discussion of the process. You are likely to avoid talking about the difficulties that you had and the areas of your work that you feel are still unresolved if you want a good mark. Some would argue that it is only by exploring and understanding the *process* that we can learn about the final *product*. Third, the students in a review might not want to question the work of their colleagues because they are aware that their comments might influence the tutors' views. So marking can reduce learning potential by stifling students into a lack of participation. Marking the work can imply that the tutor has 'the answer' (which is rubbish by the way!) – which can also leave students less likely to volunteer their own opinions.

The reality

It is likely that your review will be a combination of learning and assessment. Then, however, the final assessment of work (that which results in marks) is not anonymous. In most other disciplines anonymity is obligatory. It is easy to see how personal opinions, characters and relationships between staff and students could inadvertently affect assessment.

Researchers have suggested that if reviews are removed from the marking system perhaps they can take on a more educational role (Hall Jones, 1996). But then doesn't the review just become another form of tutorial? What will then fulfill the valid functions of the traditional review?

You can learn from reviews in many ways and can cover many different skills and subject areas. In the final review it might be too late to apply specific feedback to your work, but general principles about architectural design, construction etc. can be noted and applied to future work. Feedback could also cover presentation techniques, both in terms of your work and your physical and vocal presentation. You can learn a great deal by participating in other people's reviews and by engaging in discussion so always look at it as an integral part of the course, not as an independent event. The review fulfills different functions for you at different stages in your academic career, from seeking support and approval from others to self-validation. Whatever stage, there are many techniques that you can use to make the most of the review as a learning experience.

Learning from your own review

'A review that was really useful was when I was entering a competition. I explained the terms of the competition to the audience and asked what aspects they thought I should change and what areas needed more work. They knew I only had another two days, so it was all geared to that. I also got them to help me make a decision on the positioning of another building on the site. It felt like we were all working together.' *RS*

'You need constructive criticism – this needs to be positive as well as negative. We all need encouragement.'
Practising architect

Asking for feedback

Ask your audience specific questions about your work during or at the end of your presentation. If there is something which you are unsure of, or a decision which is proving particularly difficult, ask for other views on the matter.

Receiving criticism

Hopefully, you will have been interesting enough in your presentation to provoke discussion around your work. Your audience should offer their observations, comments and criticism, and might ask you questions.

If you are going to learn from the audience's feedback you need to learn to accept criticism. This is not always as easy as it sounds. It will help if you acknowledge imperfection and don't ever expect to have got it just right. As Anthony (1991: 35–36) quotes of a tutor, 'Completing a

'Particularly at the interims you get lots of feedback, but it's difficult not to take it personally.' *Second year student*

'When [students] hang up their work, they feel they are hanging up a part of themselves. I think if we acknowledged [this] we actually might talk about it quite differently.' *Tutor (Anthony, 1991: 107)*

project is an illusion. With experience, we just get better at creating that illusion. In other words, it's never perfect – just a better approximation.' Don't be intimidated if you seem to be receiving a lot of criticism: sometimes a harsh review is a reflection of a good design!

Listening

How to listen

At the review you are so close to your work and the effort that has gone into it that it's easy to find yourself on the defensive. You have to be able to explain your ideas and often you will be expected to justify the decisions that went into your work. But explaining why you did something is very different from defending that decision to the death. The point here is that if you listen defensively, without properly considering what is being said, you could miss useful suggestions. You should concentrate on getting precise information, understanding a problem or proposition and being stimulated into thinking of new ideas, rather than finding fault or just listening to be polite.

Paraphrasing

Check that you have understood what is being said by repeating it in another way and asking if you have understood correctly. Paraphrasing can be helpful:

- **when precise understanding is vital** – e.g. someone is explaining the principles of a construction detail to you.
- **when you are not sure that you have understood** – playing back what you understood the speaker to say so that you can address the area of difficulty instead of having to guess at what you didn't understand.

- **when you are sure you have not under-stood!** – do not simply say 'I don't under-stand, could you repeat that?' Instead, say what you think the speaker could have meant.
- **before you express a judgement about what is being put forward** – it's easy to pass judgement without thinking through what is being proposed. Paraphrasing will give you time to try to understand that position more fully before you respond and it will give the speaker time to restate his or her position more clearly if necessary. Often disagreement comes from misunderstanding.
- **before responding to a question** – if a question is being used to obtain information or to clarify understanding it is fair enough to respond immediately. If you suspect that the purpose of the question is more devious or hostile you might want to find out the true purpose of the question. You can avoid traps by using paraphrase or by simply asking the speaker why he or she wants to know.

(see Nolan, 1989: 188–189)

What to listen to

When it comes to feedback, only you can be the judge of what is relevant and valid. Feedback is often contradictory. Whatever people say, it is only their opinion. It is your work and you have to decide what goes and what doesn't. There is no definitive right and wrong. Quality can usually be recognized by the majority, but there will always be someone who disagrees. And who is to say that the majority is 'right'? You should not necessarily discount the extreme view, such as that taken by architect Jean Cocteau:

> 'Listen carefully to first criticisms of your work. Note just what it is about your work that critics don't like – then cultivate it. That's the part of your work that's individual and worth keeping.'
> (Anthony, 1991: 75)

Even if you don't want to be this radical, it is worth remembering to have, as one tutor put it, the courage of your own convictions.

Responding to ideas in sketches

Take some paper to your review so that when someone offers an idea or comment **'you can respond by sketching your interpretation'** (see cartoon 24) of what they have said. Use tracing paper to draw over your presentation as people make comments.

Recording the event

You are bound to forget half of what has been said either because you are nervous, or because so many points have been covered. Ask a friend in the audience to make notes on the feedback that you receive. Before the review you could ask your tutors if they would write down their comments so that they are clear and you can refer to them later. Try using 'review sheets' for this purpose; the example shown was devised for student use (see Review Sheet).

Another way to record the feedback is to use a tape recorder so that you can listen to the whole thing over again. Even better, **'video the event. It will be embarrassing'** (see cartoon 25) but it will alert you to aspects of your presentation. Do you really do that with your mouth? **'Were you listening constructively?'** (see cartoon 26). Are there comments you missed? Surely you don't mumble and stand in front of your drawings! Next time you might avoid some of those things.

It went well, but you didn't learn anything

For some people, the review will appear to go well just because they have the gift-of-the-gab or have produced a beautiful model/set of drawings

Cartoon 24
'... you can respond by sketching your interpretation...'

Review sheet

Date:

Your name:

Project title:

Interim/final review (delete as appropriate)

Observers' comments: (ask a friend to record comments made in the review)

....
....
....
....
....
....

Your comments: (look back on the review comments)

....
....
....
....
....

Self-assessment anticipated grade:

Tutors' comments:

....
....

Evaluation:

Concept:	V. Good	Good	Average	Poor	Fail
Development:	V. Good	Good	Average	Poor	Fail
Oral Presentation:	V. Good	Good	Average	Poor	Fail
Graphic:	V. Good	Good	Average	Poor	Fail
Models:	V. Good	Good	Average	Poor	Fail

Actual grade:

Cartoon 25
'. . . video the event. It will be embarrassing . . .'

Cartoon 26
'Were you listening constructively?'

etc. It can be frustrating to watch, especially if the tutors appear to be seduced by the presentation and don't seem to study the content of the work. Even tutors have been known to admit that, '...occasionally some (tutors) get carried away by the eloquence of a presentation plus beautiful drawings and say "in spite of what we have asked for, this is so good, we're going to give you an A".' (Wilkin, 1999)

Research has shown how graphic presentation can influence judgement of design quality. In a study by Lowe, critics were presented with a set of seven schemes all re-drawn using the same materials and conventions. Without presentation differences to hang their criticism on, the tutors felt unable to assess the relative value of design work! (Hall Jones, 1996)

Not everyone will be seduced by exceptional graphic and vocal presentation skills or excessive use of jargon. The real test is still to ask the question, 'Am I learning from the review?' You might be someone who can fob-off criticism with a convincing-sounding explanation, but while you are busy talking, you are probably not listening. Have you taken the time to think about the feedback being offered? Have you checked your understanding?

Checklist

- Ask your audience to address specific points.
- Don't be defensive about your work.
- Listen constructively.
- Use paraphrasing.
- Record the event in some way.
- Don't let your talking get in the way of your listening and learning.

Learning from other reviews

Observing

Before you can participate you need to pay attention to the presentations and discussions. Let's

'You can sometimes learn from others – that's why you need to sit and listen to all the other presentations.'
Second year student

'You can see other work and get ideas.'
Final year student

face it, if you just sit at the back of the group and daydream the day is going to be incredibly long and boring. By trying to understand, you will develop your skills in critical analysis and your understanding of architecture. Make sure you can actually see what is being talked about. Don't be afraid to go up to the work and have a closer look. Study presentation techniques and note which are effective in review situations.

Listening

As you listen to the presenter and discussion, your head will be filled with associations and connections and even completely unrelated thoughts like 'What am I going to do with those Brussels sprouts?' Your thoughts will cover more than the words that you are listening to because humans think so much faster than they speak. Speech is typically delivered at a rate of 150 words a minute, whereas your thoughts will whizz through an estimated 800–1000 words a minute (Nolan, 1989). You have to battle through all of this to try to understand and interpret what the presenter is saying. Try making keyword notes about your thoughts and associations so that you can come back to them later and continue listening to what is being said.

Use the appropriate type of listening. If you haven't understood the work presented, you can't offer constructive feedback. Waiting to speak is not listening.

Offering constructive criticism

Participating in a review as part of the audience means offering your thoughts, comments and ideas and also asking questions for further clarification when necessary. Any old participation will not do. Collaboration is what we need; this means that all participants are working towards a common goal. As mentioned previously, it is difficult to receive feedback if it isn't offered within a supportive environment. That does not mean that you cannot challenge what you have heard and seen, but any challenge should be within a supportive framework so that the presenter does not become defensive and unable to listen.

Diagram 3 shows the importance of both 'challenge' and 'support'.

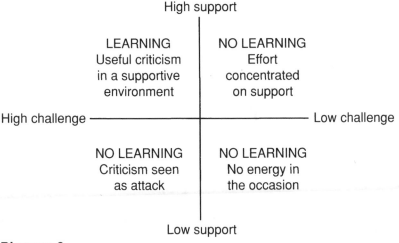

High support

| LEARNING
Useful criticism
in a supportive
environment | NO LEARNING
Effort
concentrated
on support |

High challenge ——————————————— Low challenge

| NO LEARNING
Criticism seen
as attack | NO LEARNING
No energy in
the occasion |

Low support

Diagram 3
Challenge and support

Think back to one of your reviews where you felt that the criticism offered was constructive. What made it constructive? What did the person who was giving the feedback do to make you feel that you could accept their views?

There are a few rules to bear in mind when offering feedback to someone else:

• **Identify something** *specific* **you like about the project presented.** We all need to be told when we are doing well and yet this is rare.

- **Express negative criticism as** *specific* **changes and ideas for action.** It's easier to work with specific ideas than general comments.
- **Explain the purpose of any questions you ask.** It's easy to interpret an unexplained question as an attack.

Checklist

- Make sure you can hear and see the presentation.
- Make keyword notes as you listen.
- Check that you are not just waiting to speak or listening to find fault.
- Offer constructive criticism.
- Be specific in your feedback.
- Explain the purpose of your questions.

Who can you learn from?

Tutors and students

'Tutors could try to spark discussion more than they do.' *Final year student*

Everyone can make a contribution to discussion and debate. Tutors are extremely pleased if you join in; it is very hard to be the only voice. The tutors can learn and gain valuable insight from you. Each one of us has different experiences and valuable memories to draw on. If you contribute to the discussion, the learning process becomes a collaboration between the tutors and the students (and less like a classroom). Tutors often try to encourage discussion by picking up on interesting issues but they can't force you to speak. Don't be afraid of looking stupid; if you don't understand something fully, the chances are that half of the rest of the audience won't understand either. When it comes to speaking up, remember that your views are as valid as everyone else's.

'Students become their own greatest critics.' (see cartoon 27). *Third year student (Wilkin, 1999)*

A tutor who has seen your work right through its development might not have a great deal to add in the way of feedback. You might feel that it is their role to stick up for you in your review. Sometimes you will be surprised by their lack of support, so be prepared! They might want to make sure you can stand up for yourself. Other tutors might try to explain or defend your work if your ideas are being misunderstood. Tutors who have not seen your work before could have entirely different views from the tutor that you have been meeting regularly. It is difficult to accept that views which conflict with those of your own tutor, or views which prioritize issues differently can be equally valid. It is the variety of views that leads to the variety of solutions and, ultimately, to the variety in our architectural environment. The world would be a very dull place if everyone thought like you!

Visiting critics

'External critics can be a good thing because they have fresh eyes, not having seen what you've been doing. Then again it can also be bad that they don't really know what you've been doing.' *Final year student*

'Criticism is sometimes levelled without much apparent regard for the student's growth, as educators and renowned practitioners parade their own talents verbally.' *(Cuff, 1991)*

'It would be good if they [reviews] digressed to general points and had a thread of broader intellectual discussion that runs across the work so it's less personal and there is less criticism in the negative sense of the word.' *Final year student*

Visitors might be practitioners, tutors from other schools, experts in the relevant subject, clients or building users etc. If the visiting critics have not been involved in the project during its development, there is more chance that they will have misunderstood some aspect of the brief, or interpreted certain points differently. Students and ex-students we interviewed had all experienced the visiting critic who was '**more concerned about "massaging their ego" and looking clever**' (see cartoon 28) than giving constructive feedback. Having said all of this, you will also meet visiting critics who are worth their weight in gold. They could see the project and your work in such a different way to you and your tutor, that they fill you with inspiration, breathing new life into your work. Listen before you dismiss!

Occasionally, clients and users will be present at your review. Their viewpoint will be extremely

Cartoon 27
'Students become their own greatest critics'

Cartoon 28
'... more concerned about "massaging their ego" and looking clever'

valuable and possibly very different to the student and tutor view. Don't dismiss these people as 'not understanding architecture' – it is their 'real' views that are so valuable.

Tutors and students in other years

Make time to sit in on reviews held in other years. You can adopt the role of visiting critic and try to understand the work you see for the first time. Stretch your skills in critical analysis.

Learning from discussion

Discussion is a vital learning tool. It can expand to include wider issues associated with work presented and to architecture in general. By listening to discussion and contributing to debate, you can further develop your own views and critical thinking about architecture which will feed back into your own work, improving and enriching it.

Where does your forte lie?

'Not being a stellar designer doesn't mean that you are a failure or that you're no good. Everybody in medicine doesn't have to end up being a surgeon ... there are many other forms of medical practice that are equally important and respected. The same thing happens in architecture once you start practicing *(sic)*. There are many other elements of the practice that are equally as important and respected in design. But most schools are clearly centred on design. That I know is a problem.'
Cesar Pelli (Anthony, 1991: 93)

Do you find that you just aren't cut out for reviews? Or that reviews focus on design and presentation skills and you don't seem to be able to find what it takes to be a good designer or presenter? Do not despair!

First of all, students develop skills at different rates. You might not 'get it' now, but if you hang in there, you might just find that everything falls into place later and you become a brilliant designer! Many students can describe a wonderful time when everything seemed to 'click'.

Secondly, you might not feel that design is your forte but it takes a great deal more than good design skills to be a good architect. The majority of a practising architect's time is spent doing anything but design. The world of practice moved away from this idea of the lone architect as 'baumeister' (master builder) long ago. You should be able to develop skills in a variety of areas; perhaps you are the organized type who facilitates the design team allowing it to function effectively. Increasingly, schools are recognizing these and other important skills and are allowing them to have an impact on final grades. It is becoming easier to specialize in your area of expertise.

Remember that grades neither ensure nor destroy your future career!

Summary

- Reviews can provide feedback on your work and on your presentation techniques.
- You can learn from your own review if you are prepared to listen to feedback rather than being defensive about your work.
- Criticism should be given in a supportive environment.
- You can develop your skills in critical analysis and your understanding of architecture by observing and participating in the review discussion.

Alternative reviews: 5

5 Alternative reviews

Synopsis

The guide now describes some examples of alternative review formats which you can implement. We take the opportunity to share the experiences of the Leicester and Sheffield Schools of Architecture in which a number of alternative review formats were explored. Most have been tried at other schools around the country and worldwide and are regular components of the review repertoire. Alternative reviews are offered here as a way to foster more appropriate attitudes and skills for today's architectural profession as well as improving learning.

Take control

Student life has changed considerably in the approach to the new millennium. There are a lot more of you, often paying fees, and in return you have gained more power in your choice of course and conditions of study. The balance of power has shifted (at least some way) from professionals (teachers) to clients (students).

A similar shift in power is being called for in the architectural profession. It has often been said that a good client is as important to a good building as a good architect. Today, clients are gradually becoming more involved in the whole design process. **This is more than simply a shift in power; it is the nurturing of a creative partnership.**

How is this shift being addressed in architectural education? It has always been claimed that the review provided the practice needed for interaction with clients and users. Yet the traditional review rarely encourages a creative partnership (Wilkin, 1999). The CUDE research project set out to address concerns that across the construction industry, relations with clients and building users were not what they ought to be. Architects, in particular, were accused of a remote arrogance. At the Sheffield and Leicester Schools of Architecture, independent educational advisors investigated how the attitudes of architects might be formed through their education. Both found that they had many criticisms of the traditional review process. In an attempt to tackle this problem, a number of alternative review formats and preparatory workshops were developed.

Alternative reviews

The descriptions that follow explain how to set up a selection of 'alternative reviews'. Most of these have been tried at Sheffield and Leicester Schools, and some have been found in relevant literature. You can set up many of these yourself or persuade your tutors to try them. These are ideas to build upon. These developments are still evolving and have not been tested as yet by more than anecdotal feedback. Some are only marginally different, some are radically different, none is new and the list is not comprehensive. Most can be applied to group as well as individual presentations. We hope that the alternatives presented will encourage you to '**work with your tutors to develop other options**' (see cartoon 29). **You can have an influence on your education and most tutors will welcome it.**

Cartoon 29
'... work with your tutors to develop other options.'

Setting up your own reviews

'I actually had fun listening to my friends speak and address not only the tutor but also all the rest of us...'
Second year student

'[I enjoyed] the lack of tutors' incessant boring waffle. The fact we got involved.' *Second year student*

The wonderful thing about student-led reviews is that you can set them up alongside existing reviews. They have the added benefit of not needing much tutor input at a time when class sizes are growing and there seems to be fewer tutors. You don't need to get tutors involved if you don't want to. You probably already participate in reviews like these on an informal basis, chatting with friends about your work and so on. Getting more people involved can be really valuable. You can use the following guide to set up most of the alternatives described in the rest of the chapter.

- **Plan the structure of the review**. How long is each student going to present? Are you going to present individually or in groups? When are you going to start, and when will you have breaks?
- **Structure the feedback**. Agree specific questions appropriate to the project, e.g. use of materials, children's safety. Who will give feedback to the presenter?
- **Organize a location**. If it's a completely student-led review, then 'it **doesn't have to be in your school**' (see cartoon 30).
- **Inform everyone.** Give everyone a copy of the structure of the review in advance.
- **Appoint a timekeeper**. Students tend to be much stricter than tutors!
- **Tutors' role**. The role of tutors, if they are involved (and willing), is to manage the process. Alternatively students from higher up the school could be facilitators. Tutors might sit at the back and find out what it is like!
- **Arrange seats**. Arrange seats in a single line semi-circle around the presentation area.
- **Organize feedback forms**. Print a form for each student. As their work is being reviewed, ask someone to record the comments.

Cartoon 30
'... it doesn't have to be in your school'

'We stayed totally awake and interactive for three hours ... Constructive, interesting and useful – I felt I learned a lot from other people's crits too.'
Second year student

'The whole thing seems to work a lot better without a tutor (sorry).'
Second year student

'Tutors need a chance to say something to stop us sitting at the back, chatting, smoking and making paper planes.' *Tutor*

We used the student-led review at Sheffield to promote teamworking and communication skills. Most of the students involved really enjoyed it. Judging from feedback, the main advantages of setting up student-led reviews is that they encourage lots of participation, allow you to share problems with others who have been working on the same project, and are less boring! Some students were sure that the process had been better without input from tutors but the tutors felt frustrated at having their tongues tied!

Role-play review

This is a way of trying to see the work through the eyes of non-architects.

- **'Choose members of the audience to represent the views of client, developer, planner, etc'** (see cartoon 31).
- Presentation by student(s).
- Review panel prepares questions from the point of view of their role.
- Allow time for questions from each viewpoint and discussion.

At Sheffield, workshops were held to develop communication skills. Students then met with either the client, user or expert for their project who asked questions from their specific viewpoint. This helped students to represent these specific roles in the reviews. Students found this approach valuable as it allowed them to appreciate that there are different viewpoints, often contradictory, which an architect has to take into account with perception and sensitivity.

Cartoon 31
'Choose members of the audience to represent the views of client,
developer, planner, etc.'

Introduce real clients and users

'[Reviews] should be more about "learning to present your ideas to lay-people.' *Practising architect*

'This was very helpful as presentation to a different group is distinctly different to presentation to architects.' *Second year student*

Perhaps the most obvious way to practise inter-action with clients and users is to introduce them into the design and review process. This is something that is requested repeatedly by students (Wilkin 1999) but is surprisingly difficult to organize. Provided that the contributions of lay reviewers and tutors are both valued, '**it broadens the debate**' (see cartoon 32) to include issues that are important to non-architects.

In one project at Sheffield at which clients and users were present at interim and final reviews, students felt they learned the importance of the architect's relationship with the client/user and how to communicate with, and present to, non-architects.

Make the tutor do the work

- Brief a tutor on your work.
- Get the tutor to present your work to the review panel and note what was communi-cated and what was missed.

This model mirrors what often happens in practice where only senior partners present the work of their staff to clients. You could alterna-tively ask another student to present your work. It encourages you to describe your work briefly and clearly.

Exhibition review

Projects are often presented in practice in the absence of the architect. Competition entries, in particular, must 'speak for themselves'. Projects of broad public concern are frequently exhibited to get feedback. Communicating clearly to lay-people is important, especially if they are to become effective participants in the design process.

Cartoon 32
'... it broadens the debate'

- Plan a presentation (drawings, models, slides, multimedia, etc.) in a coherent and logical manner to be understood by lay-people unfamiliar with reading architectural drawings.
- Tutors examine the work without students present.

When Leicester held an exhibition review, it worked well but tutors did question some students about specific points to ensure they were not disadvantaged in assessment.

Private view

Planning an exhibition either in your school, a local gallery, community centre, etc. allows you to discuss work and ideas in an informal atmosphere. This gives you the freedom to choose who you talk to about what, and for how long. Seeing the work as a whole, rather than a series of individual presentations, can encourage broad debate about architecture.

- Plan an opening night and **'invite members of the public'** (see cartoon 33).
- Each exhibit should be accompanied by a written explanation.
- Ask everyone briefly to view all of the projects.
- Spend time discussing the work with members of the public.
- Write down feedback, highlighting particular points with examples. Alternatively, assign a small group to each exhibit to give feedback.

Selective review

This format need not include student presentations. Tutors can focus on the key issues in the project.

- Each student exhibits their work.

Cartoon 33
'... invite members of the public'

- Tutors look at all the work and select examples of drawings, models, etc. that illustrate the main points.
- Tutors explain the main points to the whole group, illustrating the points with the selected examples, followed by discussion.
- Short individual reviews can follow, if necessary, which can then concentrate on issues specific to each project.

See your work through others' eyes

This is good way of testing whether or not your architectural intentions have been met. Understanding how people react to different spaces can help you in your future work.

- Pick an important space or aspect of your design.
- Record how you intend people to react to that space.
- Ask others to record their responses to the space.
- Compare your intentions with the responses.

Meeting review

In a meeting format everyone is involved equally and everyone is expected to contribute. This is a useful approach for small groups of up to ten for tutorials and five for reviews.

- Everyone presents their key ideas in two or three minutes.
- Each person then states the issues they want to discuss.
- Arrange these in priority order as an agenda for the meeting.
- Give time for discussion on issues highlighted in the agenda.

Brochure review

This simulates a presentation to a small committee.

* Prepare your drawings, photographs of site and models, etc. and a short report in the form of a brochure.
* Provide copies for everyone.
* Allow time for all to read and annotate the brochures.
* Give time for discussion with everyone able to see a brochure and each other face-to-face.

Model review

Architects assume that clients and the public understand their drawings but very often they do not and we rarely discover misunderstandings until it is too late. Some cultures in the world never draw. Models are far more accessible to most people. This format allows only models.

Students did this at Leicester for a complete project and quickly developed a whole range of alternative modelling techniques to cover the early stages of design as well as presentation. These early stages are where it is most important that clients understand what is being considered and from which they are largely excluded by traditional approaches.

Lecture review

Think you could give a better lecture than your tutors? A short lecture presentation encourages you to investigate widely but then to distil the key points in difficult subjects; useful for planning *any* presentation. A series of short sharp lecture presentations can be very effective and can stimulate you to 'learn to learn'.

- Allocate or select research topics.
- Distil your key points from all of the information.
- Pick visual material to reinforce your key points.
- Plan your presentations to identify what you are trying to communicate and to what audience.
- Prepare a short talk virtually word-for-word and edit it down to three minutes.
- Give the lecture. You might find you can speak confidently without reading.
- Get the audience to ask questions and give feedback.

Workshops at Leicester were run on preparing a lecture, using the voice effectively, and preparing and using overhead transparencies. These also covered how to deal with questions and criticism and encouraging openness to new ideas. Staff were impressed by the difference a little basic training could make but some students, particularly those from overseas, found giving a lecture intimidating and some, who needed the voice training most, missed the session.

IT review

An IT review can range from a few 'slides' to a multimedia presentation combining slides with video, sound, animation and even interaction. You can reach a larger audience by using a projector.

At the Leicester School, a design project was combined with a course in computer presentation skills. In successive weeks, first year students learned the basics of computing, two-dimensional drawing, three-dimensional modelling, and presentation systems. By the end of the fourth week, they presented their design ideas on screen including enlarging particular details to focus on issues under discussion; everybody could see relevant details and join in. Accessibility for students to sufficient systems needs careful planning. This high-stress project was one which students rated highly.

Video-conference review

This is a technology that is developing rapidly and becoming more affordable. Video-conferencing is a powerful tool for presentation and interactive discussion and is being used increasingly in practice. It provides an opportunity for more frequent interactive communication combining visual and verbal material.

A video-conferencing review requires particular skills which need practice. The technology will develop but the principles remain. At the time of writing, there are two main systems: room sessions like a meeting or lecture, and desktop sessions like a telephone call. Systems permit the transfer of video, sound and digital files. Each medium can be pre-recorded or transmitted live.

For 'room sessions', limitations include that the technology is not yet widely available, it can be unreliable, and pre-booking is usually needed. Controlling the equipment requires expertise and concentration that is difficult to combine with presenting information and usually needs help from technical staff.

Here are a few useful guidelines:

- Drawings need clear contrast, avoiding fine detail, and text must be large and clear.
- Keep quiet while somebody is speaking. Transmission is possible in only one direction at a time and needs a second or so to adjust.

- Excessive movement may appear either blurred or jerky because information has changed more rapidly than it can be transmitted.

Make them shorter and with fewer people

Huge groups and long days of reviews are not successful as a learning opportunity (Wilkin, 1999). Try persuading your tutor that you don't need to be there all day (I know you'll like this one!). Divide the group up and only stay for half a day.

Group reviews

'It would be good if they digressed to general points and had a thread of broader intellectual discussion that runs across the work so it's less personal and there is less criticism in the negative sense of the word.' *Diploma student*

This is a good way to encourage discussion of broader issues relevant to the project as a whole. It should also mean that the review panel does not need to repeat the same point again and again.

- Divide the students presenting into groups of about five people.
- The five students in one group then make their presentations one after another.
- Time is given after each group for feedback from the review panel.

Double presentation

This method has the advantage that students have to be involved in giving feedback. It's a two-way thing – the student presenting benefits from the additional feedback and the reviewer benefits from concentrating on another piece of work.

- To each student presenting (student A), allocate a reviewer (student B). Give them time to study the work before the presentation.

- Student A presents their work.
- Student B then presents their assessment of the project.
- Tutors and others may then give further feedback on the presentation.

Feedback forms

This is a useful addition to the traditional review. It avoids the situation where you forget what was said during the review.

Either:

- Put a feedback form on your presentation with specified subject areas for comment, asking everyone to make a comment and perhaps even give a grade, or
- Give each student/tutor a review sheet similar to the 'review sheet' described in Chapter 4.

Summary

- You can try alternative formats in addition to traditional reviews.
- You can suggest some alternative ideas to your tutors. They will be pleased to know you are thinking about it.
- There are many alternatives you can set up yourself.
- You can use these examples as a springboard for developing others.
- Even *small* changes that you can make to your own review could have a big impact on your learning.

Reviews and the future: 6

6 Reviews and the future

Summary

This guide has focused on traditional reviews: surviving them, getting more out of them, and developing alternatives. This final chapter suggests new directions for the future because of what is called 'the new professionalism'. Changing professional attitudes challenge us to work in a different relationship with clients. It is hoped that this guide will have taken you through a survival course and then launched you on the first steps towards more creative client participation in the design process.

Reviews and the future

There is concern across the construction industry about the poor relationship with clients – architects are fanciful, planners say 'no', builders are cowboys, quantity surveyors are killjoys, services go wrong, buildings are sick, and the professions do not talk to each other. This is not a healthy environment for an exciting, creative industry.

This distrust is so fundamental that it was decided to look at ways of fostering better relationships from where professional attitudes begin, at the start of university courses. This was the origin of the CUDE Project (Clients and Users in Design Education), to which reference has already been made.

A variety of approaches has been taken including developing live projects and working more closely with clients and users. Dr Margaret Wilkin, an educational consultant, was commissioned to examine how students became aware of client and user needs in the Leicester School. A comprehensive analysis was made of design projects, investigating how students learned to consider user needs and how they learned to communicate with clients and users. Dr Wilkin examined project briefs, how projects were introduced to students, and the content and conduct of tutorials. She found little specific reference to client and user issues and was told that they were addressed during final reviews. And so began her focus on final reviews by observation, interview and questionnaire with significant results reaching far beyond the initial issues.

An independent view

The value of this comprehensive independent study was that Dr Wilkin came with wide experience of education but with no preconceptions about architectural education. This put her initially in the place of first year students who she saw as being initiated at reviews into games without written rules; the referees (staff) knew the rules but the players (students) could only discover them by breaking them and being 'criticized'. This set up negative connotations with 'The Crit' from the outset.

Dr Wilkin argued that, given the significant proportion of staff time devoted to interim and final reviews, we should do more to engender an effective and positive learning experience. Students spent a lot of time looking at drawings too far away to see and listening to discussion they could barely hear in noisy distracting studios. Much of the discussion at reviews focused on poor aspects of poor projects, the room layout discouraged discussion, and students were reluctant to criticize one another. Finally, Dr Wilkin asked why reviews were broadly similar in style throughout three years and why no training in presentation skills was given.

Far from being the forum in which client and user attitudes could be developed positively, reviews were engendering from the outset the negative attitudes of confrontation that the CUDE study was commissioned to change. Based on the traditional academic model of defending a thesis but supposedly now simulating practice, the review was setting up an expectation of confrontation and moulding student attitudes that would sour future relationships with clients.

These were challenges that could not be ignored. We can make the excuses of 'more students, less staff, more administration, more research' but they just reinforce the need for change. This became the catalyst for developing many of the alternative reviews already described.

Old habits die hard and the review has served architectural education for over a century and so the alternative reviews replaced just some of the traditional reviews; a revolution might be needed but an evolutionary approach was adopted.

Fundamental questions

It would be difficult to compare traditional versus alternative reviews and such an analysis would miss the main point. The alternative reviews are about far more than removing negative aspects of 'the crit', saving staff time, or using new technologies. By far the most important outcome is that they aim to foster an attitude which respects clients and users as potentially creative participants in the design process.

What began as a study of information and attitude is evolving into the nurturing of 'a new professionalism' which questions almost every aspect of the review culture. Why do we do reviews? What should students get out of them? Why do we present handcrafted finished work? Why do we present drawings at all? Why do we defend rather than learn?

The ageing review, it seems, is in need of more than a facelift; it is **'facing the wrong way and using too much mouth and not enough ear'** (see cartoon 34). The next step is to develop a whole range of skills to encourage creative inter-action.

More than a facelift

If this guide helps you to prepare for reviews effectively, it has achieved its first objective of 'survival'. If it helps you to get more out of reviews, it has achieved its second objective of 'reducing confrontation'. If it encourages you to develop 'alternative reviews', that is a bonus. But if it encourages you to take **'a step towards "creative partnership"'** (see cartoon 35), it will achieve long-term investment in your future and in a better future for the design and construction industry.

Cartoon 34
'... facing the wrong way and using too much mouth and not enough ear'

Cartoon 35
'... a step towards "creative partnership"'

Bibliography

Anthony, K.H. (1991). *Design Juries on Trial – the renaissance of the design studio*. Van Nostrand Reinhold.

Cuff, D. (1991). *Architecture: the story of practice*. MIT Press.

Hall Jones, S. (1996). Crits – an examination. *Journal of Art and Design Education*, 15 (2), 33-141.

Lewis, R. K. (1998). *Architect? A candid guide to the profession*. MIT Press.

Lowe, J. B. (1969). The Appraisal of Designs. *RIBA Journal*, 76 (9), 379-80.

Nicol, D., Pilling, S., eds (2000). *Changing Architectural Education*. E & FN Spon. (in press).

Nolan, V. (1989). *The Innovator's Handbook – the skills of innovation management*. Sphere Books.

Rethinking Construction: The Report of The Construction Task Force (Egan Report, 1998). HMSO.

Schön, D. A. (1983). *The Reflective Practitioner: how professionals think in action*. Temple Smith.

Tierney, E. (1996). *How to Make Effective Presentations*. Sage.

Wilkin, M. (1999). *Reassessing the Design Project Review in Undergraduate Architectural Education with Particular Reference to Clients and Users*. An in-house report, produced for the CUDE project at The Leicester School of Architecture, De Montfort University.

Index